Adorable Animals

CHRISTINE THOMAS ALDERMAN

WORLD BOOK

This World Book edition of *Baby Harp Seals*
is published by agreement between
Black Rabbit Books and World Book, Inc.

2140 Howard Dr. West,
North Mankato, MN 56003 U.S.A.
World Book, Inc.,
180 North LaSalle St., Suite 900,
Chicago, IL 60601 U.S.A.

Marysa Storm, editor; Catherine Cates, interior designer; Grant Gould, cover designer; Omay Ayres, photo researcher

Library of Congress Control Number: 2017029600

ISBN: 978-0-7166-3438-6

Printed in China. 3/18

Image Credits

Alamy: age fotostock, 16, 24–25; All Canada Photos, 28–29; Arco Images GmbH, 13 (top); Eric Baccega, 6; imageBROKER, 13 (bttm); Juergen Sohns, 20; Kevin Schafer, 4–5; Nature Picture Library, 26 (large image); Rolf Hicker Photography, Cover; Dreamstime: Vladimir Melnik, 26 (silhouettes); en.wikipedia.org: GeographBot, 25; iStock: zanskar, 27; Newscom: Michio Hoshino, 10–11; Solent News / Splash News, 9; Shutterstock: Alexey Seafarer, 22 (bear); Ant_art, 14–15 (bkgd); Christian Musat, 23; CookiesForDevo, 31; Denis Burdin, 16–17; FloridaStock, 1, 3; Vladimir Melnik, 6–7, 19, 21, 22–23, 26, 32; yukitama, 14–15 (silhouettes)

Every effort has been made to contact copyright holders for material reproduced in this book. Any omissions will be rectified in subsequent printings if notice is given to the publisher.

CONTENTS

CHAPTER 1

A Cute and Cuddly

It's early spring in the Arctic. A baby harp seal cries out for food. The little white pup pulls itself across the ice to its mother. The mother knows its baby by its smell. It lets the pup **nurse**. The hungry pup drinks and drinks.

How Big Is a
Newborn Harp Seal?
LENGTH
LESS THAN
3
FEET
(1 meter)

Hello, World!

Harp seal pups begin life on ice. They arrive in late February to mid-March. The newborn pups are tiny compared to their mothers. But they grow quickly. Pups gain about 5 pounds (2 kilograms) a day from drinking their mothers' milk.

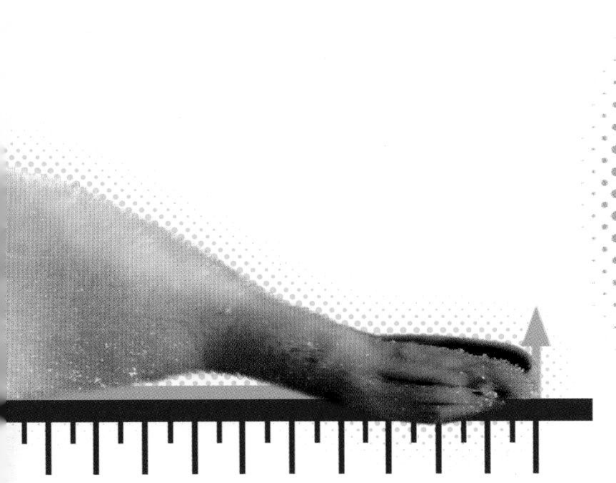

Changing Clothes

Adult harp seals spend a lot of time in water. But newborn pups cannot swim. They must stay on the ice. Their white fur helps them blend in with their surroundings. **Predators** struggle to see them. As pups learn to swim, their fur turns gray. Gray fur helps the pups blend in with the water.

BABY HARP SEAL FEATURES

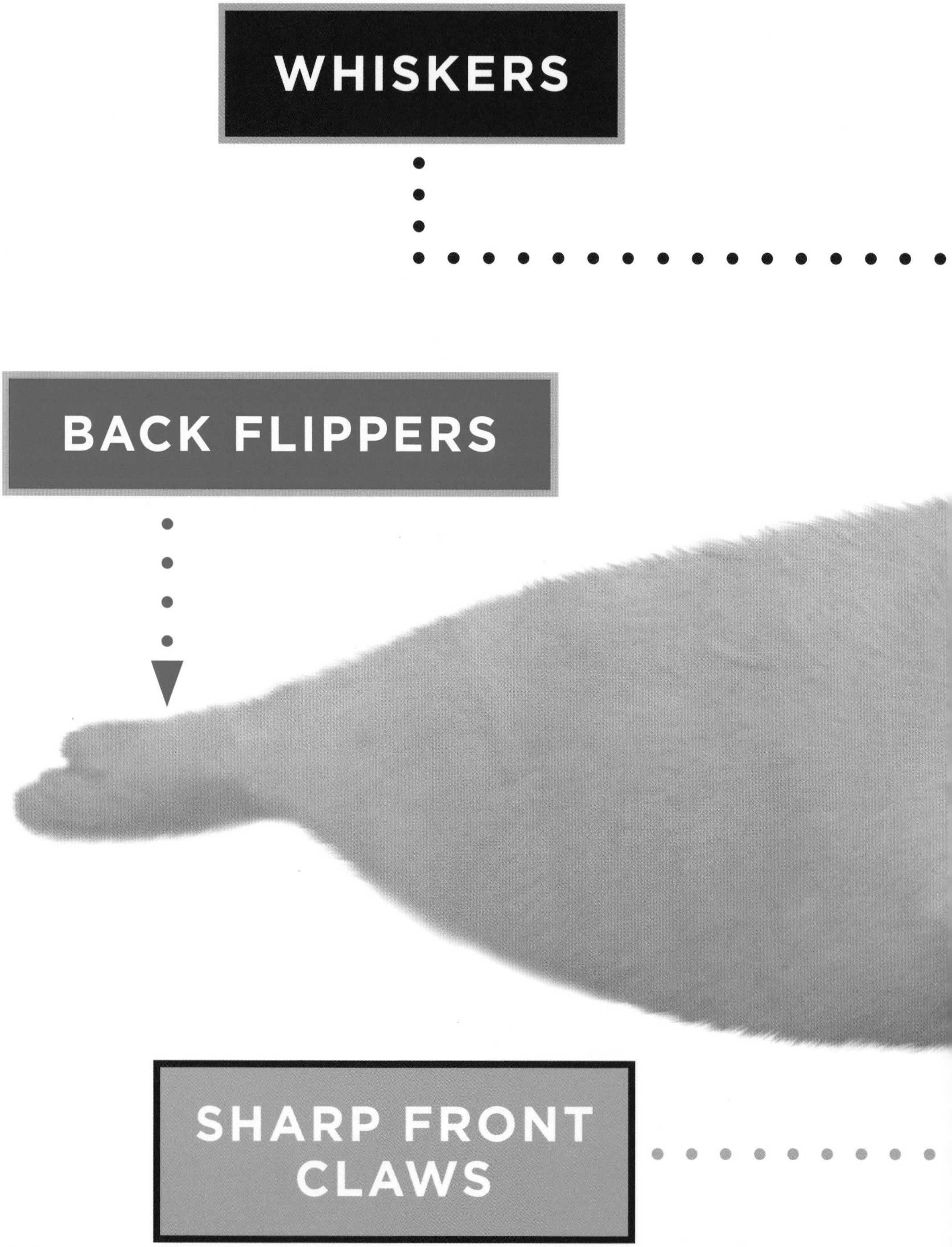

WHISKERS

BACK FLIPPERS

SHARP FRONT CLAWS

WHITE FUR
BLACK NOSE
FRONT FLIPPERS

CHAPTER 2

A Place to Call

Harp seals swim in the North Atlantic and Arctic Oceans. Groups of harp seals often travel and feed together. They go onto pack ice or land to give birth and raise their young. They often return to the same places each year.

Pack ice is a large area of ice not attached to the shore.

HARP SEAL RANGE MAP

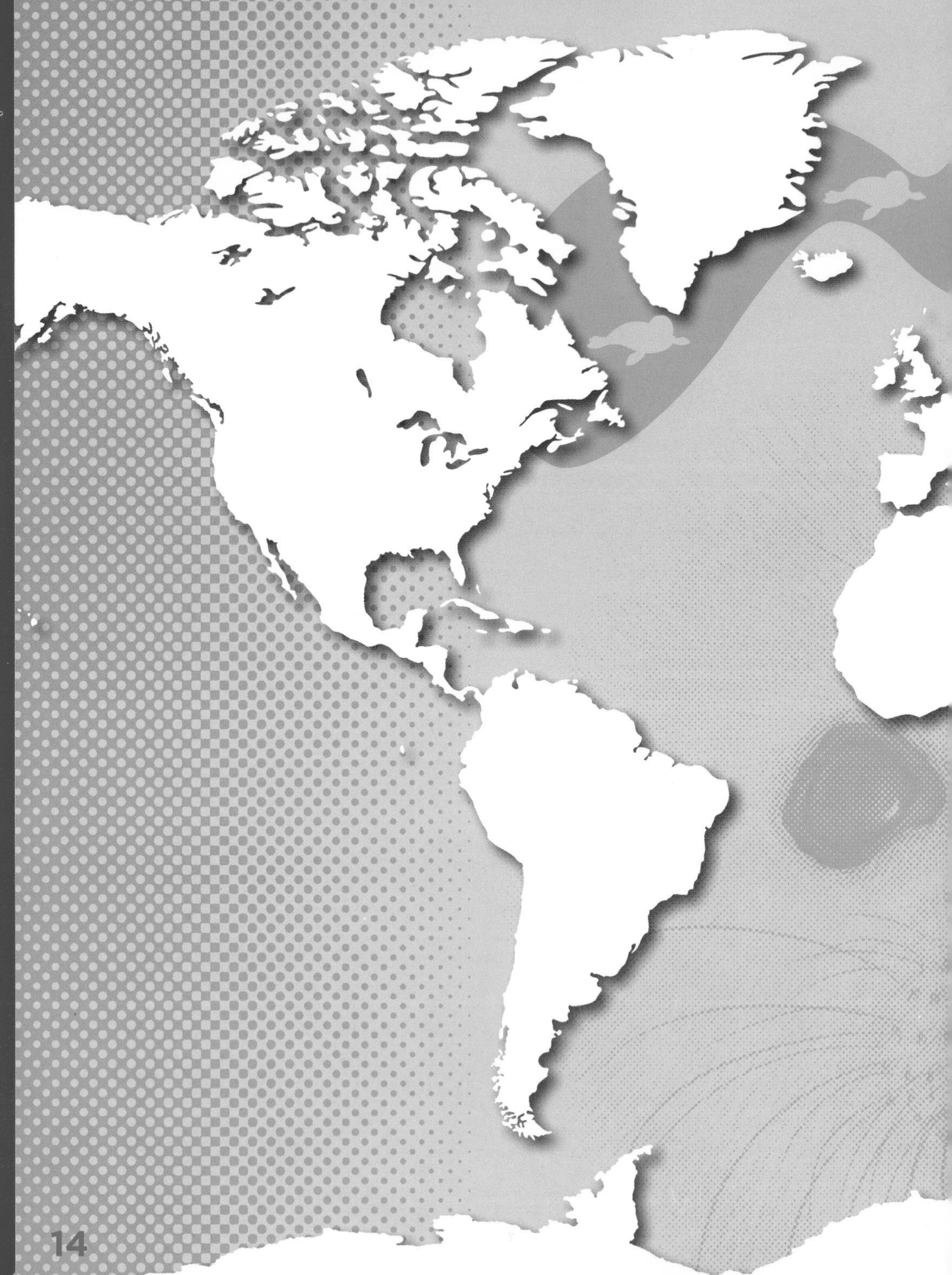

Changing Habitat

A pup's home is a dangerous place. **Climate** change is raising Earth's temperatures. Warm temperatures melt pack ice before the pups are ready to start swimming. If pack ice breaks apart too soon, pups drown. Falling ice can also hurt young seals.

CHAPTER 3

What's for Dinner?

Pups begin drinking their mothers' milk soon after they're born. The milk is about half fat. That's a good thing. Fat makes **blubber** under the pups' fur. Blubber keeps the pups warm.

Pups drink milk for about two weeks. Then their mothers leave to **mate**. They don't return. Alone on the ice, the pups can't hunt for food yet. Their blubber gives them energy.

Mother harp seals won't take care of any pups but their own.

Swimming Solo

Young pups can't live off blubber forever. They must find food. Pups teach themselves to swim and hunt. They beat their flippers on melting ice to practice swimming. Then they dive into the water and look for food. Harp seals dine mostly on fish.

Shaped for Swimming

Watch Out!

Little harp seals have big predators. Humans hunt the pups for their white fur. Polar bears prowl the ice. They eat whitecoats. Sharks and killer whales circle underwater looking for seals too.

By the Numbers

10 to 14 DAYS

HOW LONG MOTHERS NURSE THEIR PUPS

1

NUMBER OF PUPS A MOTHER HAS AT ONE TIME

about **15** minutes

how long adult harp seals can spend underwater

11½ MONTHS

how long female harp seals are **pregnant**

more than **50** percent

PERCENT OF BODY MASS PUPS LOSE AFTER THEIR MOTHERS LEAVE

30 to 35 years

LIFE SPAN

CHANGING SIZES

NEWBORN	TWO-WEEK-OLD
about 24 POUNDS (11 kg)	about 80 POUNDS (36 kg)

CHAPTER 4

Growing Up

As harp seals grow up, they learn to dive deep underwater. They become better hunters. And they develop larger spots. Eventually, marks shaped like **harps** appear on their backs.

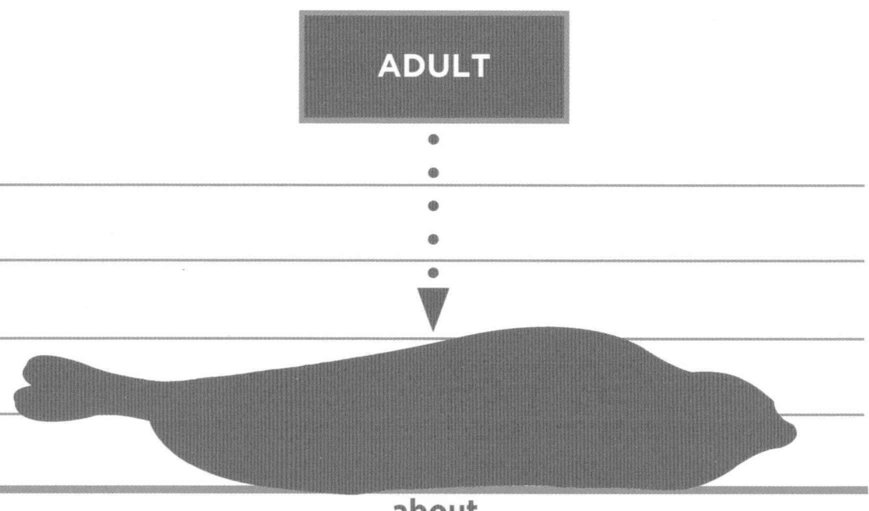

Welcome Back!

When harp seals are about five years old, they're ready to have their own babies. They return to pack ice near where they were born. The female seals find safe places to have their babies. They nurse their pups. Soon, these new pups will learn to swim and hunt.

blubber (BLUB-uhr)—the fat on whales and other large sea mammals

climate (KLAHY-mit)—the usual weather conditions in a particular place or region

harp (HARP)—a stringed instrument

mate (MAYT)—to join together to produce young

nurse (NURS)—to feed a baby or young animal with milk from the mother's body

predator (PRED-uh-tuhr)—an animal that eats other animals

pregnant (PREG-nuhnt)—carrying one or more unborn offspring in the body

sleek (SLEEK)—straight and smooth

BOOKS

King, Aven. *Harp Seals*. Ocean Friends. New York: PowerKids Press, 2016.

Meinking, Mary. *The Dangerous Lives of Harp Seals*. Stories from the Wild Animal Kingdom. Mankato, MN: Child's World, 2018.

Phillips, Dee. *Harp Seal*. Arctic Animals. New York: Bearport Publishing, 2015.

WEBSITES

Harp Seal
kids.nationalgeographic.com/animals/harp-seal/#harp-seal-closeup.jpg

Harp Seal
www.nmfs.noaa.gov/pr/species/mammals/seals/harp-seal.html

Harp Seal
www.seals-world.com/harp-seal/

INDEX